Maurice Pledger

Olivia Owl's
STICKER BOOK

Written by A.J. Wood

All About Animals

Silver Dolphin

Published in 2000 by

Silver Dolphin Books

An imprint of the Advantage Publishers Group

5880 Oberlin Drive, San Diego, CA 92121-4794

www.advantagebooksonline.com

Illustration copyright © 2000 by Maurice Pledger/Bernard Thornton Agency, London

Text and design copyright © 2000 by The Templar Company plc

ISBN 1-57145-450-0

Designed by Tracey Cunnell
Concept by Sydney Stanley

Printed in Italy by STIGE

1 2 3 4 5   00 01 02 03 04

How to use this book

On the following pages you'll find lots of sticker activities to do as you discover all about animals with Olivia Owl and her friends.

You'll find puzzles and animal picture galleries to complete, outline sticker shapes to match, and you can also make up your very own pictures by adding stickers to the colorful scenes scattered throughout the book.

Just turn to the back of the book and you'll find all the stickers you need to have lots of fun. And when you've finished, you can reuse your stickers to make new pictures or decorate your letters or notebooks.

L ook! Here is Olivia the baby owl. She lives far away in an enchanted forest and she is always looking for someone new to play with. Luckily, the forest is full of all sorts of different animals, from creatures that crawl to others that jump, swim, and run, or even fly like Olivia Owl. In fact, there are so many creatures in Olivia's forest that today she is going on an adventure to see just how many different types of animal she can find. Why don't you join her on her journey and see how many new animals friends you can discover. And don't forget to use your stickers along the way.

Olivia's favorite friends

Here is Olivia with her friends Billy Bunny, Sally Cygnet, and Dilly Dormouse. They are just three of the many different animals that Olivia knows.

Duggy Duckling

Oscar Otter

Sammy Snake

Hoppy Frog

Sophie Salmon

Belinda Butterfly

Sydney Snail

Use your stickers to fill in the pictures above with seven more animal friends. Look out for them all again later in the book.

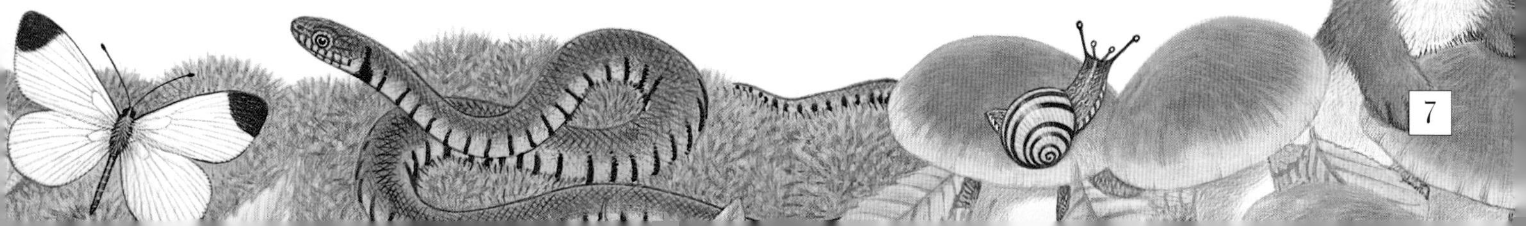

All types of animals

Some of Olivia's friends are covered in feathers, just like Olivia! They are called **birds**. Use your stickers to fill in the outline shape with Olivia's missing feathered friend.

Olivia Owl

Elly Eagle

Henry Hummingbird

Winston Woodpecker

Duggy Duckling

Jenny Wren

Some of Olivia's friends are covered in fur. They are called **mammals**. Use your stickers to fill in Olivia's missing furry friend.

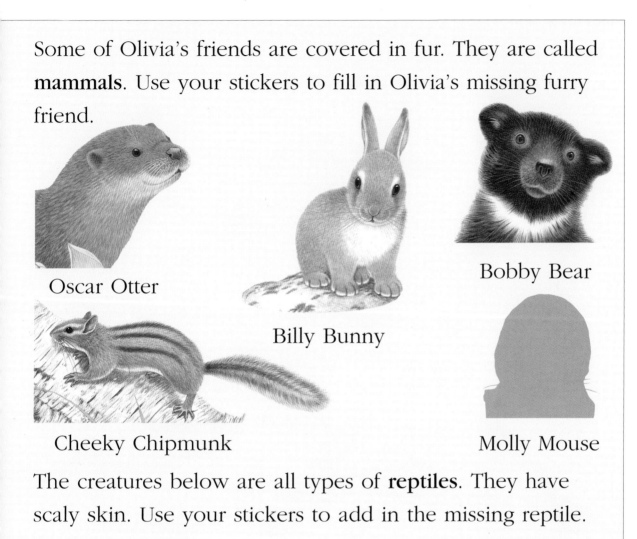

Oscar Otter

Billy Bunny

Bobby Bear

Cheeky Chipmunk

Molly Mouse

The creatures below are all types of **reptiles**. They have scaly skin. Use your stickers to add in the missing reptile.

Sammy Snake

Terri Terrapin

Lance Lizard

These creatures are covered in soft skin. They are called **amphibians**. Fill in the missing amphibian with a sticker.

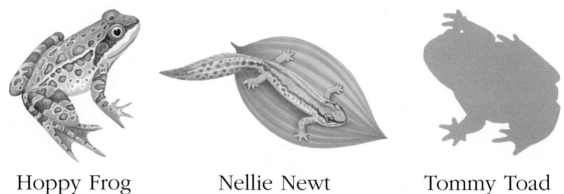

Hoppy Frog   Nellie Newt   Tommy Toad

Olivia Owl knows lots of different **fish**. Here are four of her fish friends. Use your stickers to add one more.

Spiky Stickleback

Gilly Goldfish

Sophie Salmon

Percival Pike   Penny Perch

The forest is full of different **insects**. Here are four different kinds of insects. Use your stickers to add one more.

Liv Ladybug

Buzzy Bumble Bee   Belinda Butterfly

Artie Ant   Bertie Beetle

As well as insects, Olivia has discovered all sorts of other **creepy crawlies** living in the forest. Fill in the missing one with your stickers.

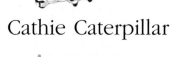

Will Wood Louse

Cathie Caterpillar

Spin Spider   Sydney Snail   Sylvia Slug

O livia knows that different kinds of animal have different kinds of skin. Some have skin covered in fur or feathers. Others have scales or shells to protect them. Help Olivia by using your stickers to fill in the pictures with the correct missing creature.

Who flies high in the sky and is covered in feathers?

Elly Eagle

Who hops by the pond and is covered in skin?

Hoppy Frog

Who leaves a silver trail and carries a hard shell on her back?

Sydney Snail

Who swims in the river and has shiny, golden scales?

Camilla Carp

Who loves honey and is covered in soft black fur?

Bobby Bear

Who lives where?

Olivia's animal friends live in all sorts of different places. Some live in the forest like Olivia. Others live in the meadow nearby. Use your stickers to fill in the missing animal that lives in each different place.

Forest

Who lives in the forest with Freddy Fox and Winnie Wolf?

Winston Woodpecker

Riverbank

Who lives on the riverbank with Oscar Otter?

Sally Cygnet

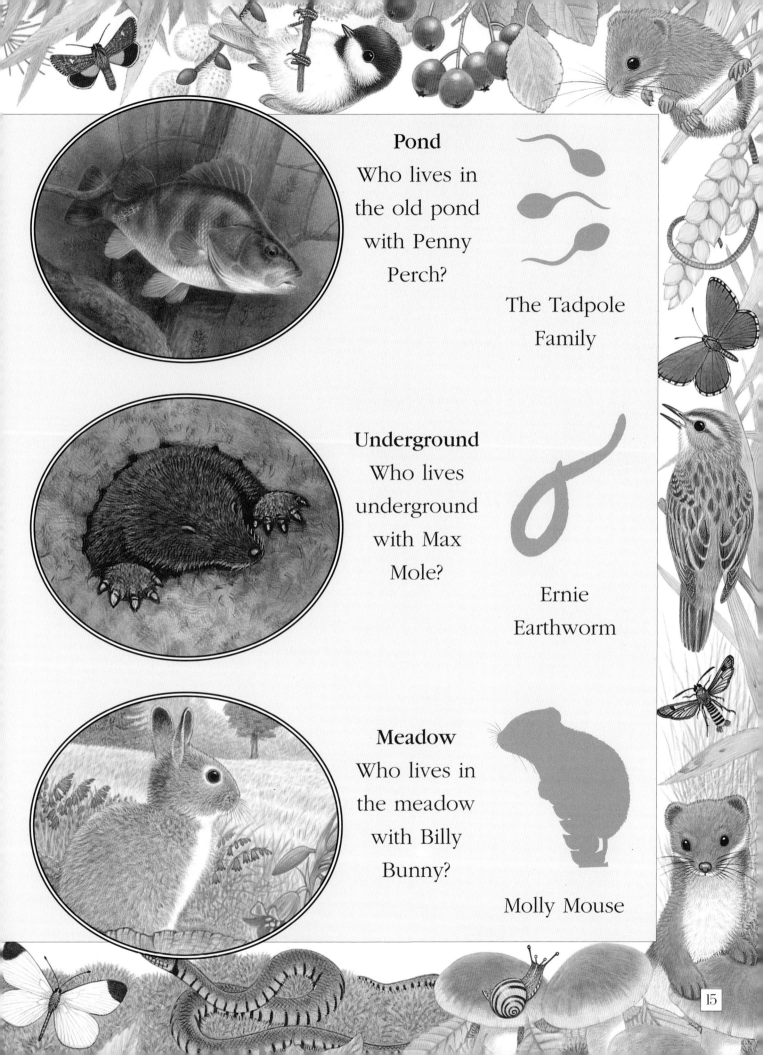

Pond

Who lives in the old pond with Penny Perch?

The Tadpole Family

Underground

Who lives underground with Max Mole?

Ernie Earthworm

Meadow

Who lives in the meadow with Billy Bunny?

Molly Mouse

Nighttime creatures

Some animals only like to come out to play when it gets dark. Use your stickers to fill in the pictures of four creatures who come out when darkness falls.

Beth Badger

Barnaby Bat

Freddy Fox

Minnie Moth

L ots of animals are out and about in the daytime. Look! Olivia has found Billy Bunny and Bobby Bear playing in the sunny meadow. Use your stickers to add Sally Squirrel, Molly Mouse, Curly Quail, and two butterflies to the picture as well.

Wintertime

Billy Bunny is looking for his friend Bobby Bear, but he cannot find him anywhere. That's because Bobby is one of many animals that go to sleep in the winter.

Bobby Bear

Sammy Snake

It's a special kind of sleep called **hibernation**, and it helps animals to survive the cold weather. Use your stickers to fill in the pictures of four animals that go to sleep when winter comes.

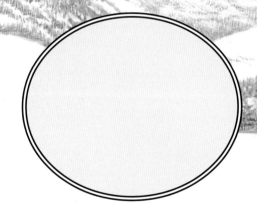

Buzzy Bumblebee

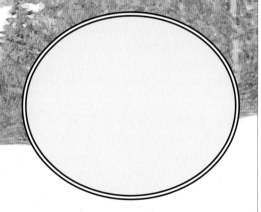

Beth Badger

A nimals move around in all sorts of different ways. Look at the animals in this picture. How do they move? Now use your stickers to add a crawling snail, some hopping grasshoppers, a scurrying mouse, and two flying dragonflies to the picture.

Use your stickers to add seven different types of animals to join Olivia Owl and her friends in this picture of the forest.

Feathered friends

Olivia Owl knows lots of different birds. Here she is with her brother Ozzy Owl and their friend Curly Quail. Use your stickers to put four more of their feathered friends in the picture—Jenny Wren, Hillary Hummingbird, Elly Eagle, and Winston Woodpecker. Which is your favorite feathered friend?

Which bird do you think owns these furry feet? Why, it's Olivia Owl of course! Use your stickers to fill in the outline shape with a picture of Olivia, then see if you can help her find the missing birds to match the other pictures of different beaks and feet.

Which bird has a long, thin beak to help her drink nectar from flowers?

Hillary Hummingbird

Which bird has webbed feet to help her swim through the water?

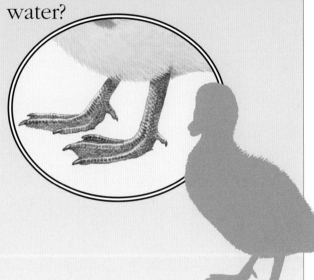

Daisy Duckling

Which bird uses her tiny feet to grip tree branches?

Goldy Goldcrest

Which bird uses her long sharp beak to catch fish?

Eliza Egret

O livia Owl is covered in fluffy brown feathers, but some birds have feathers in all sorts of bright colors. Here is William Wood Duck and his friend Katie Kingfisher. Use your stickers to add four more colorful birds to the picture—Betty Bluetit, Finny Finch, Hillary Hummingbird, and Swifty Swallow.

Who lays eggs?

All birds lay eggs, but some other creatures lay eggs as well. First use your stickers to put Sally Cygnet and some eggs in this nest that Olivia has found by the river. Then fill in the pictures with four other animals that lay eggs.

Liz Lizard

Sarah Snake

Tilly Turtle

Sophie Salmon

35

Furry friends

Here is Olivia with two of her favorite furry friends–Oscar Otter and Dilly Dormouse. Now use your stickers to fill in the pictures with five more mammals that live with Olivia in her forest home.

Ricky Racoon

Bobby Bear

Winnie Wolf

Cheeky Chipmunk

Sammy Skunk

37

Who lives where?

Olivia and some of her friends have found some honeybees living in a hive in the old tree stump. Olivia knows that there are other animals living in homes all over the forest. See if you can help her by putting your stickers of the missing animals back in their homes on the opposite page.

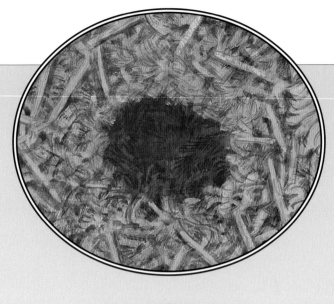

Sally Squirrel lives in a nest of twigs made high in a tree. It is called a **drey**.

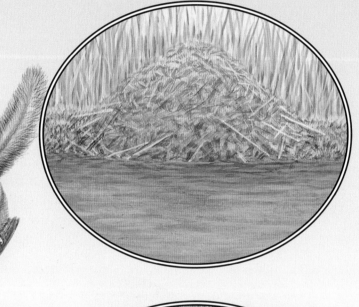

Becky Beaver lives in a home in the middle of the river. It is called a **lodge**.

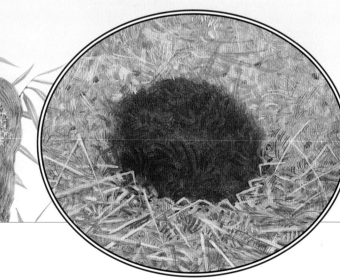

Beth Badger digs her home under the ground. It is called a **sett**.

L ook whom Olivia has found playing in the forest. Can you see two birds and two mammals? What other type of creature can you see? Now use your stickers to put four more furry friends in the picture—Billy Bunny, Cheeky Chipmunk, Molly Mouse, and Oscar Otter.

Some of Olivia Owl's mammal friends have interesting heads and tails. See if you can help Olivia find the missing animals on your sticker sheet to match the different heads and tails.

Becky Beaver has a wide, flat tail. It is shaped like a paddle.

Molly Mouse's tail is long and thin. It is covered in soft, pink skin.

Freddy Fox has a big, furry tail. It is called a **brush**.

Mac the Mountain Goat has short, pointed horns.

Duke Deer has big, knobbly horns. They are called **antlers**.

Use your stickers to make up your own picture of Olivia and her animal friends playing down by the riverbank. How many different creatures can you see?

Reptile rundown

Did you notice Sammy Snake and Lance Lizard in the river bank scene? They are both reptiles. Use your stickers to fill in the pictures with three of their reptile relatives.

Tilly Turtle   Terri Terrapin   Liz Lizard

Whom else might Olivia find down by the river? It's Hoppy Frog. Use your stickers to put Hoppy in the picture, then add three more amphibians to the scene– Tommy Toad, Sal Salamander, and Nellie Newt.

ome of Olivia's friends are covered in lovely patterns. See if you can help Olivia fill in the missing animals to match the different patterns using your stickers.

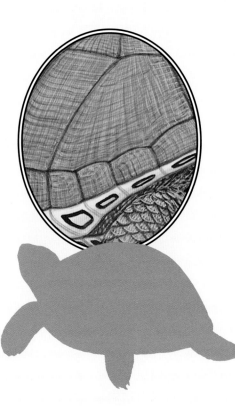

Tom Tortoise can hide his whole body beneath his patterned shell.

Curly Quail's patterned feathers help him to hide in the long grass.

This **swallowtail butterfly** has a bright pattern on its wings.

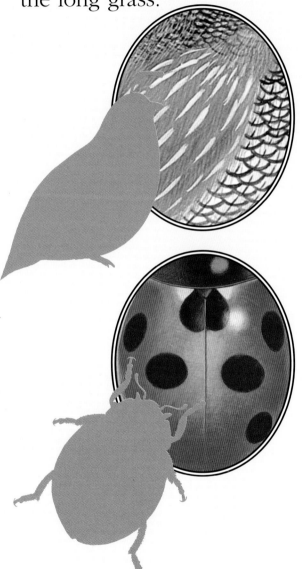

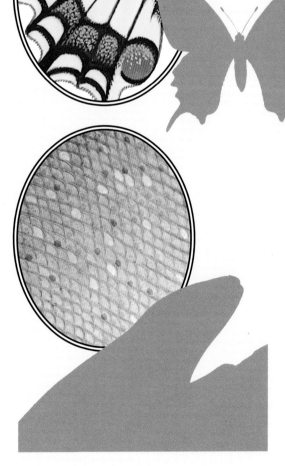

Liv Ladybug has a pattern of black spots on her back.

Liz Lizard's scaly skin is covered in a spotty pattern.

Fish friends

Lots of different fish live in the river that runs through the forest where Olivia Owl lives. Here is Tracy Trout looking for her friends! Use your stickers to fill in the outline shapes of four more fish friends.

Who else lives underwater?

Olivia Owl knows that, apart from fish, there are other creatures who live underwater. Use your stickers to fill in the pictures with four more underwater creatures.

Dragonfly Larva

Water Snail

Tadpole

Water Beetle

S ophie Salmon spends all her time swimming up and down the river. Can you think of any other animals that are good at swimming? Use your stickers to fill in the pictures with four more super swimmers.

Oscar Otter

Becky Beaver

Duggy Duckling

Hoppy Frog

Interesting insects

Look! Olivia has found three interesting insects down by the riverbank—Liv Ladybug and two beautiful butterflies. Use your stickers to add a bee, a beetle, a dragonfly, and four scurrying ants to the picture.

How many different flying insects can you name? Here is Buzzy Bee flying from flower to flower. Use your stickers to fill the pictures with four more insects that can fly.

Fly

Mayfly   Butterfly   Moth

A creepy-crawly collection!

Olivia and her friends Sally Cygnet and Oscar Otter are hunting for creepy-crawlies down by the old log. Use your stickers to fill in the outline shapes with four creepy-crawlies that they might find.

Earthworm

Slug

Spider

Millipede

W hom has Olivia found crawling around on the forest floor? Why, it's Sydney Snail! Now use your stickers to add a caterpillar, a centipede, a wood louse, and another snail to the scene as well.

Make up your own picture of the sunny meadow by adding stickers of different insects and creepy-crawlies.

Parents and babies

Here are five different babies. Match them up with their parents by filling in the missing creatures with the right sticker from your sheet.

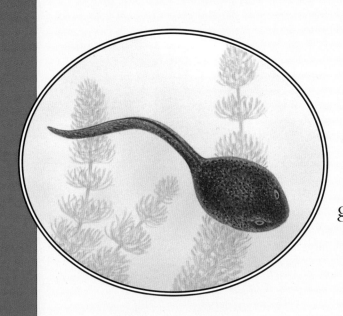

This wriggly **tadpole** will grow up to be a big, green, hopping **frog**.

This fluffy **duckling** will grow proper feathers and become a fine **duck**.

This crawly **caterpillar** will make a cocoon and emerge as a beautiful **butterfly**.

This strange creature is called a **nymph**. It will grow up to be a dazzling **dragonfly**.

This baby owlet will grow up to be a big, strong **barn owl**. Tu-whit! Tu-whoo!

Now to finish the book make up your own picture of Olivia and all her many animals friends.

How to use your stickers

Look for the page numbers on the sticker sheets. They will help you find the right stickers for the different activities in this book.

Peel each sticker carefully from its backing sheet and stick it in the right place in the book. You can use the stickers again and again if you remember to treat them carefully.

Sheets 6 and 12 contains lots of stickers for you to make up your own pictures. You can use them with the big scenes in the book. Or you could draw your own picture of Olivia's forest home and stick them on that!

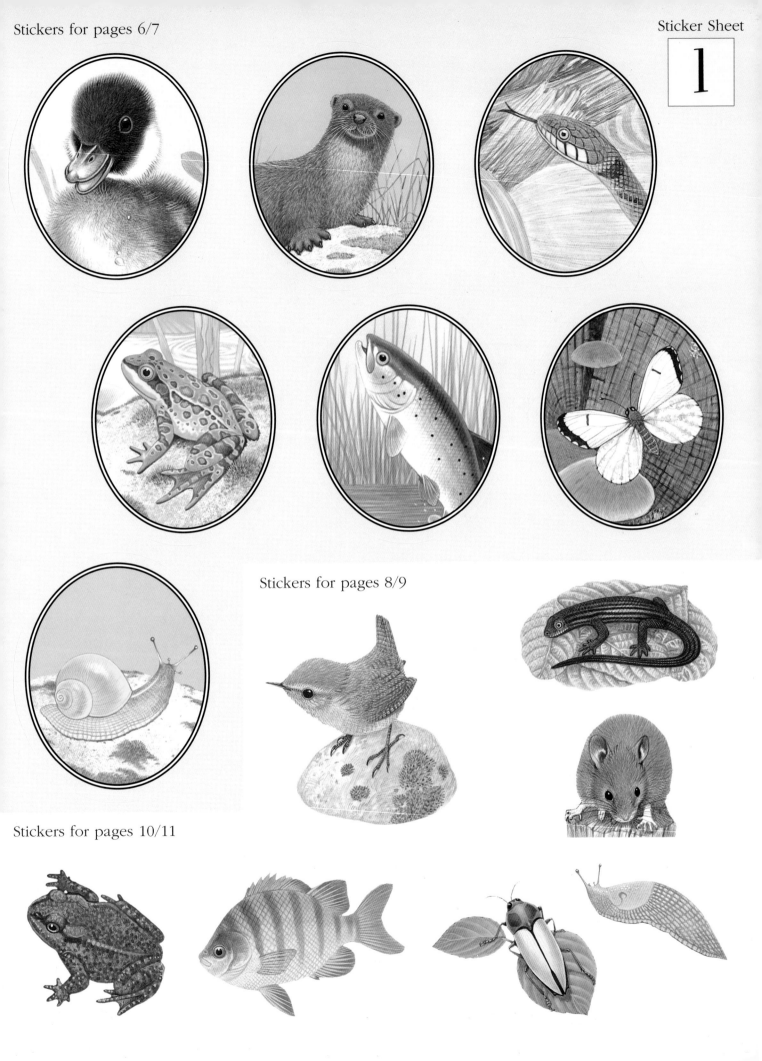

Stickers for pages 6/7

Sticker Sheet

1

Stickers for pages 8/9

Stickers for pages 10/11

Stickers for pages 12/13

Stickers for pages 14/15

Stickers for pages 16/17

Stickers for pages 18/19

Stickers for pages 20/21

Stickers for pages 22/23

Stickers for page 24/25 can be found on Sticker Sheet 6

Stickers for pages 26/27

Olivia for page 30

Stickers for pages 28/29

Stickers for pages 30/31

Stickers for pages 32/33

Sally Cygnet for page 35

Stickers for pages 34/35

Stickers for pages 44/45 – The Riverbank

Sticker for page 35   Stickers for pages 36/37

Stickers for pages 38/39

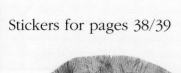

Sticker for pages 40/41

Stickers for pages 40/41

Stickers for pages 42/43

Stickers for pages 44/45 can be found on Sticker Sheet 6

Stickers for pages 46/47

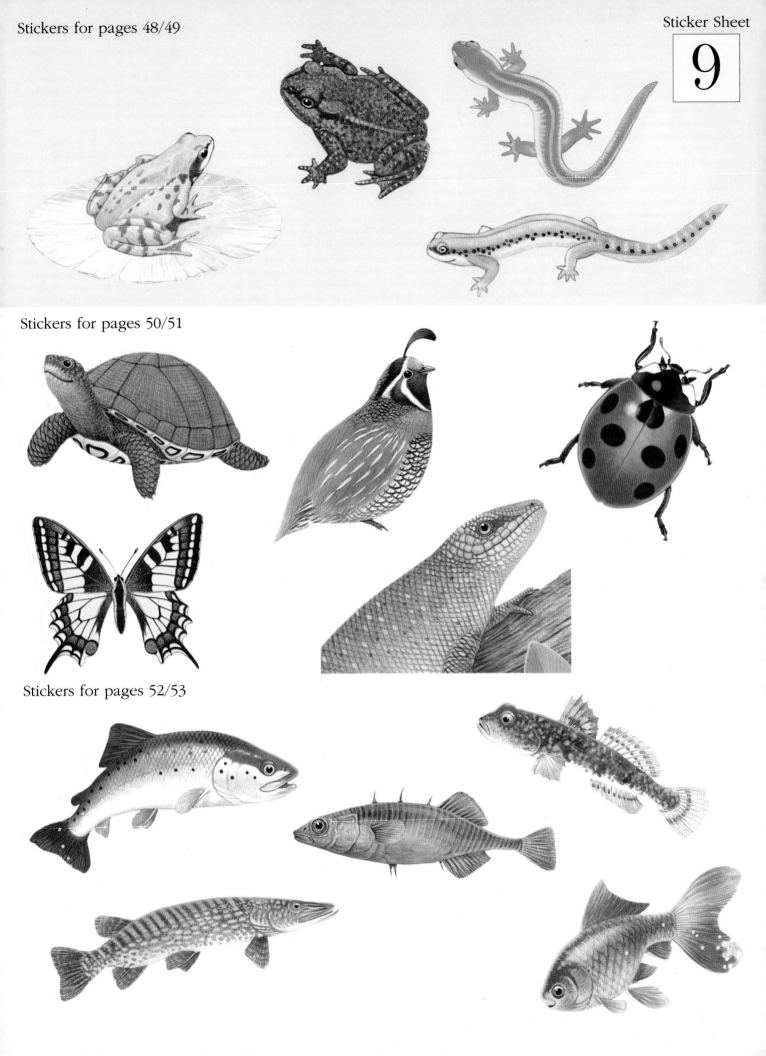

Stickers for pages 48/49

Stickers for pages 50/51

Stickers for pages 52/53

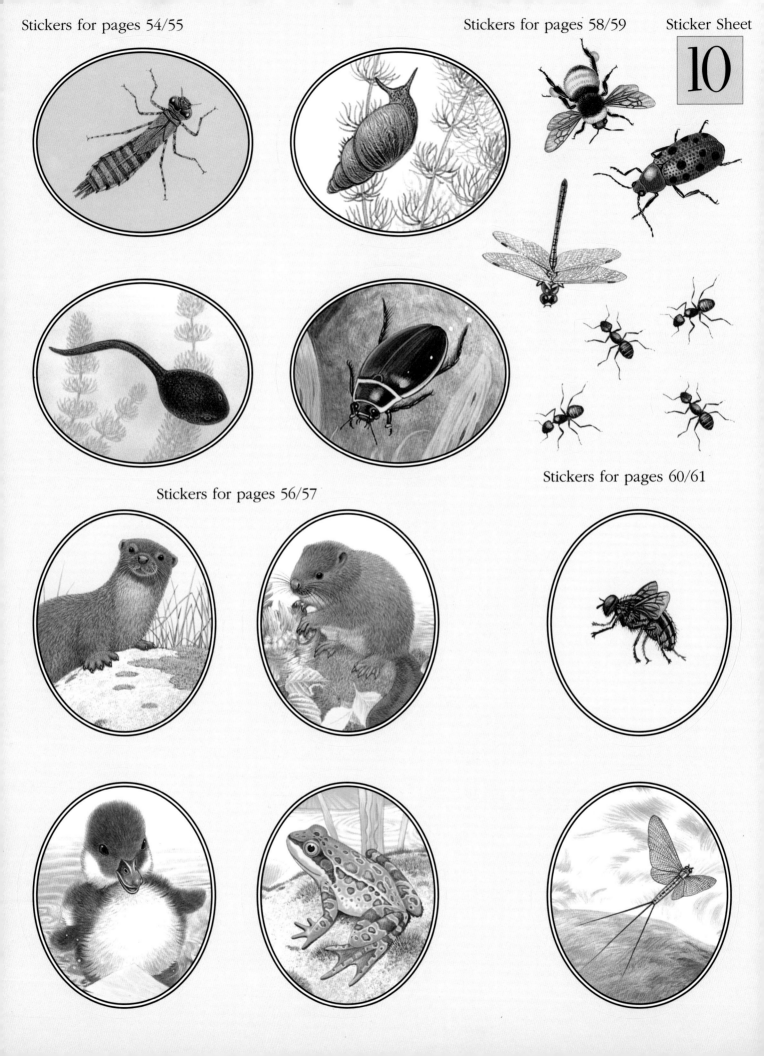

Stickers for pages 54/55

Stickers for pages 58/59

Sticker Sheet

10

Stickers for pages 56/57

Stickers for pages 60/61

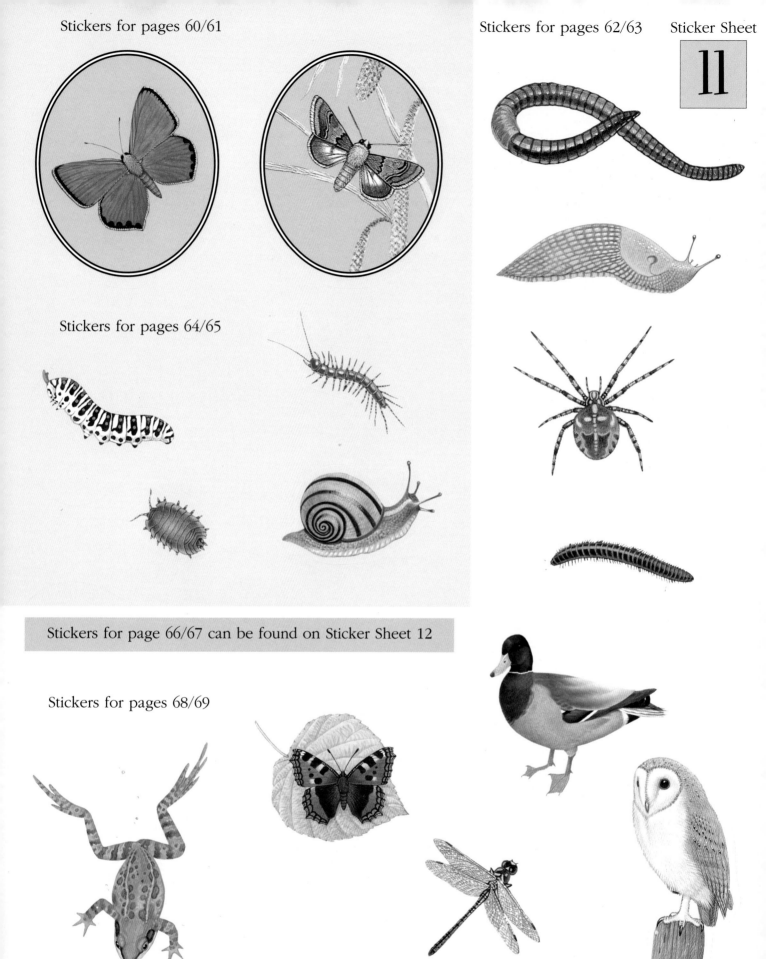

Stickers for pages 60/61

Stickers for pages 62/63   Sticker Sheet

11

Stickers for pages 64/65

Stickers for page 66/67 can be found on Sticker Sheet 12

Stickers for pages 68/69

Stickers for page 70/71 can be found on Sticker Sheet 12

Stickers for pages 66/67 – The Meadow

Stickers for pages 70/71 – Olivia and her many animal friends